DINO-ROARS!

DIPLODOCUS

By Shalini Vallepur

BookLife PUBLISHING

©2019
BookLife Publishing Ltd.
King's Lynn
Norfolk PE30 4LS

Printed in Malaysia.

A catalogue record for this book is available from the British Library.

ISBN: 978-1-78637-739-5

Written by:
Shalini Vallepur

Edited by:
Madeline Tyler

Designed by:
Danielle Jones

Photocredits:

Images are courtesy of Shutterstock.com.
With thanks to Getty Images, Thinkstock Photo and iStockphoto.

Front Cover - Luis Louro 2 - I Wei Huang. 4 - paleontologist natural, Luis Louro. 5 - Janaken2012, Ira_Photo, FrameAngel, Mega Pixel. 6 - GOLFX, Sever180, Bjoern Wylezich, Moha El-Jaw. 7 - Elnur. 8 – Lumena. 9 - Freer, Christos Georghiou, . 10 - Smithsonian Institution from United States [No restrictions], via Wikimedia Commons, Shor [Public domain], via Wikimedia Commons. 11 - Art by A. Atuchin. Published by D. Cary Woodruff, Thomas D. Carr, Glenn W. Storrs, Katja Waskow, John B. Scannella, Klara K. Nordén & John P. Wilson. [CC BY 4.0 (https://creativecommons.org/licenses/by/4.0)], via Wikimedia Commons. 12 - U.S. National Park Service, restoration/cleanup by Matt Holly [Public domain], via Wikimedia Commons. 13 -paulaphoto, Photo by Michael Overton. [CC BY-SA 2.5 (https://creativecommons.org/licenses/by-sa/2.5)], via Wikimedia Commons, Newtonian, K Steve Cope. 14 - Vasilyev Alexandr. 15 - Wlad74, Julia Kuznetsova. 16 - Freer Marysha. 17 - N-sky, cjchiker. 18–19 - Sgoran cakmazovic, LegART. 20 - Et3e. 21 - Gelpi, Orla, Catmando. 22 - Heinrich Harder (1858-1935) [Public domain], via Wikimedia Commons. 23 - Luis Louro, Linda Bucklin, Marysha.

CONTENTS

Page 4 Welcome to the Dino-Trek!

Page 6 What Are Fossils?

Page 8 Diplodocus

Page 10 Palaeontologists of the Past

Page 12 Let's Dig

Page 14 Greedy Eaters

Page 18 Crack That Whip

Page 20 Follow the Footsteps

Page 22 Think Again

Page 23 End of the Trek

Page 24 Glossary and Index

Words that look like **this** can be found in the glossary on page 24.

WELCOME TO THE DINO-TREK!

Check out page six to learn all about dinosaur fossils!

It's time to see some dinosaurs! You will become a palaeontologist and go on an adventure looking for dinosaur fossils.

Every palaeontologist needs a good set of tools.

Magnifying glass

Brush

Spade

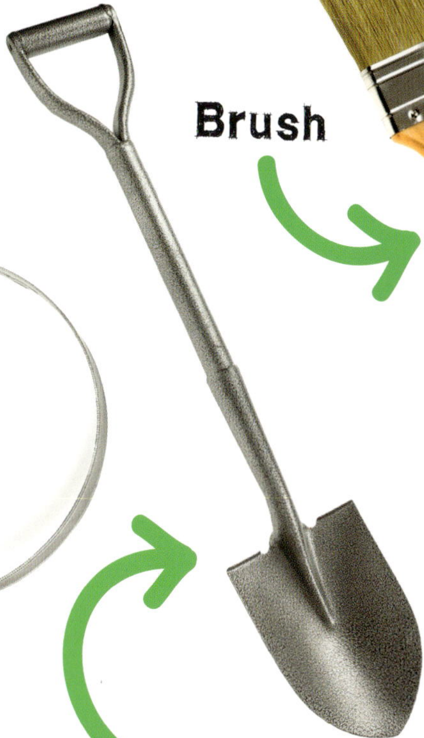

Gloves

A palaeontologist is a scientist who studies what life on Earth was like before we humans came around. They go on **excavations** looking for fossils.

WHAT ARE FOSSILS?

A fossil is made when an animal or plant is **preserved** in rock. The hard parts, such as bone or shell, are left behind. They leave a shape in the rock for us to study.

Palaeontologists study lots of different types of fossil, from animals and plants to bacteria.

Dinosaur fossils are millions of years old. Palaeontologists must be very careful not to break or damage fossils. They wear gloves to handle fossils and gently brush away dirt.

When a fossil is found, it is taken back to a laboratory.

DIPLODOCUS

Have you ever seen a picture of Diplodocus? It had a huge neck and a long tail.

Diplodocus was a type of dinosaur called a sauropod.

Diplodocus lived around 153 million years ago. From the end of its **snout** to the tip of its tail, Diplodocus could grow to around 30 metres long.

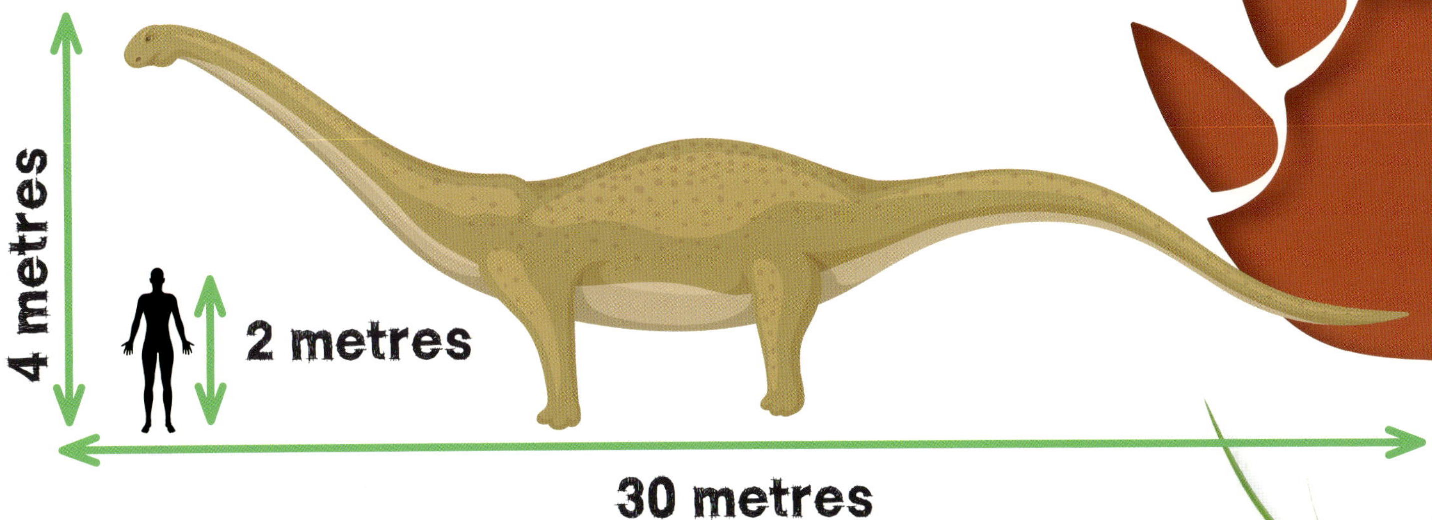

PALAEONTOLOGISTS OF THE PAST

Palaeontologists Earl Douglass and Samuel Williston first discovered Diplodocus fossils in 1877. It must have been amazing to find such a big fossil.

Andrew the Diplodocus

In 2010, a **juvenile** Diplodocus fossil was found. He was named Andrew. Although Andrew was young, he was already a massive six metres long!

LET'S DIG

We have to find a good **site** to excavate. Palaeontologists can't just dig wherever they want to. We can use fossil maps that show where fossils have been found before.

We can think about Diplodocus's **habitat** too. It is believed that Diplodocus lived in **plains** and areas of **woodland** where the US is today.

GREEDY EATERS

Is there something buried in the ground? It needs to be gently removed using a spade so we can clean it and get a closer look.

We found a Diplodocus skull! Can you see how the teeth are at the front of the skull? These teeth are perfect for stripping the leaves off a branch. This tells us that Diplodocus was a **herbivore**.

Palaeontologists think that Diplodocus removed leaves from plants and trees in one single swipe. Diplodocus was very big, so it had to eat a lot of plants.

It is thought that Diplodocus swallowed stones to smash up plants in its stomach. Stones that are swallowed like this are called gastroliths.

CRACK THAT WHIP

If you look closely, you might notice that Diplodocus's tail is longer than its neck. But why was its tail so long?

Diplodocus used its long tail to help it balance its neck and body to stand up straight. It could also whip its tail to make terrifyingly loud booming noises.

Fossils show the tail was made of around 80 bones.

FOLLOW THE FOOTSTEPS

It might be hard to see, but this is a dinosaur fossil trackway. These trackways are usually footprints that have been preserved over time. This one looks like it could have been made by Diplodocus.

We think that Diplodocus travelled around in **herds**. Sauropod trackways have been found that show that adult and juvenile sauropods stayed together.

Why do you think Diplodocus travelled in herds?

THINK AGAIN

Sometimes palaeontologists get things wrong at first. Many people believed that Diplodocus crawled around like a lizard with its belly on the floor. Palaeontologists now know that this isn't true.

END OF THE TREK

There's still a lot to discover as a palaeontologist. New fossils are being excavated and studied all the time. Maybe you could be the next palaeontologist to discover a sauropod as delightful as Diplodocus!

GLOSSARY

bacteria tiny living things, which are too small to see, that can cause diseases

excavations careful removals of earth from an area in order to uncover buried remains or ruins

habitat the natural home in which animals or plants live

herbivore an animal that only eats plants

herds large groups of animals that live together

juvenile young and not grown up yet

laboratory a room or building used by scientists to carry out experiments and research

plains large areas of flat land with a few trees

preserved kept in its original form

site a place where something is

snout the front part of an animals head that sticks out, including its nose and mouth

woodland an area of land covered in plants

INDEX

bones 6, 15, 19
brushes 5, 7
excavations 5, 12–13
fossils 4–7, 10–12, 19–20, 23
gloves 5, 7, 13
juveniles 11, 21
magnifying glasses 5
necks 8, 18–19
palaeontologists 4–7, 10, 12, 16, 22–23
plants 6, 15–17
sauropods 8, 21, 23
skulls 15
spades 5, 12, 14
tails 8–9, 18–19
teeth 15